AN INFORMEI

WALKING WITH GOD

Fr Joseph Hattie OMI

FAMILY PUBLICATIONS

An Informed Conscience: Walking With God
Joseph Hattie OMI

ISBN 1-871217-37-7

First published 1991 (revised 1999) by the
Office of Marriage and Family Formation,
Archdiocese of Vancouver, Canada

© Joseph Hattie OMI, 1991, 1999
revisions in this edition © Family Publications, 2002
CNS photo by Irene C Michel
Scripture quotations from the RSV, Catholic Edition

Published in the United Kingdom by
Family Publications
6a King Street
Oxford OX2 6DF
www.familypublications.co.uk

TABLE OF CONTENTS

PREFACE 5

I INTRODUCTION 6

II INFORMING ONE'S CONSCIENCE:
    SOME INITIAL FACTS 7

III THE SEARCH FOR WHAT IS TRUE
    A Introduction 13
    B Assistance in the Search (1) 18
    C Assistance in the Search (2) 20
    D Use of your Free Will 22

IV AN INFORMED CONSCIENCE
    A The Person 23
    B The Person's Qualities 26
    C The Person's Inner Core 28
    D Love's Foundation: The Person 30
    E Teaching Children 31
    F God 33
    G How God Helps Externally 36
    H The Conscience Informed 41

V CONCLUSION 45

NOTES 47

SUGGESTED FURTHER READING 48

PREFACE

The primary objectives of the book are:

- To examine explicitly what it means to inform one's conscience.
- To give guidelines for informing one's conscience in a responsible way.
- To help develop an attitude of humility toward the truth, so that one will seek to discover it rather than create it.
- To introduce the concept of objective reality.
- To make manifest the importance of one's decisions and how to make decisions in harmony with God.
- To explain why the Church teaches us to follow an *informed* conscience.

The secondary objectives are thus:

- To help engaged and married couples appreciate how much they can help one another, both in the formation of their individual consciences and those of their children. This is truly a work of love.
- To help parents realize that, since they are the primary teachers of their children, and thus the first to assist in the formation of their children's conscience, it is important that they understand what these responsibilities entail.
- To help priests and the laity to understand properly and put into practice the Church's teaching in this area.

I

INTRODUCTION

Have you ever considered what you might have done if it had been you in the Garden of Eden rather than Adam and Eve? Do you think you might have done better? Do you think you might have been wiser, especially when conversing with Satan?

Probably we like to think we would have done better or have been wiser than Adam and Eve. Such thoughts, however, should lead us to ask the obvious question: *How* could we have done better? The answer of course is: by doing what Adam and Eve failed to do. They should have taken the time to discover whether the stranger in the garden had actually told them the truth, before they acted on what he told them. This effort is called *informing one's conscience*.

It is important always to inform your conscience before you act, so that you will choose what is good and avoid what is evil. To appreciate this, reflect on the fact that there were drastic consequences when Adam and Eve acted without informing their consciences. Throughout the rest of your life, you will have many opportunities to do better than Adam and Eve. You should pray daily for the grace to do so.

II

INFORMING ONE'S CONSCIENCE: SOME INITIAL FACTS

In the first three chapters of *Genesis*, the story of Creation and Man's fall, God gives us many points to reflect upon when considering the importance of the decisions we make. I would like to expand briefly upon a few of them here. If you have the time, you might like to read through these chapters in full for yourself.

From this story of Man's creation and fall into sin, the following basic facts about each one of us can be deduced:

1. You are a gift

> "God created man in his own image, in the image of God he created him; male and female he created them."

Man is the only creature on this earth that God created *for itself*.[1] Therefore each human being is firstly a gift (from God) *to one's self*. This means that we have been given complete freedom over our selves, the freedom to give ourselves to whomever we choose.

> "And when the woman saw that the tree was good for food, and that it was a delight to the eyes, and that the tree was to be desired to make one wise, she took of its fruit and ate."

At the base of every one of our free decisions, we make a choice to give ourselves to someone. Ultimately, we give ourselves either to God or to Satan through each decision we make; and the good or bad choices we make in life will determine our eternal destiny.

The life of Adam and Eve teaches us this most important lesson. We should remember that each human being is called to become a total gift, freely given, to God and his neighbour. It is when we refuse to give of ourselves that we turn away from God.

2. You are of great value

> "Then God said, 'Let us make man in our image, after our likeness; and let them have dominion over the fish of the sea, and over the birds of the air, and over the cattle, and over all the earth, and over every creeping thing that creeps upon the earth'."

Our decisions are important for another reason. As God's special creations, we have a very great value. When we give ourselves as a gift to another, we are not giving away a few pence worth of chemicals, but rather the most precious of God's creatures in this world. We know too that if we give something good to God, then He will do many more good things with it. It is part of the mystery of his love that He wants us to cooperate with Him in doing good for others. For example, when Christ fed the five thousand people in the wilderness, He used the five loaves and two fish given to him by the young boy (cf. Mt 14:17–21). In our own time, Christ has physically and spiritually fed millions through his Church and through individuals like Mother Teresa, who gave the gift of herself to Him. We are called to give ourselves to God, so that we may be his instruments for doing good in the world.

On the other hand, since Satan's intentions are to bring about the *absence* of the good that should be (which we call 'evil'), he needs good gifts in order to do so. And the better the gifts which are given to him, the more evil he can do. Certainly the very best gift one can give to him is one's self; with a person he can do much evil. History is replete with outstanding examples of Satan's power to bring about evil through human agents. Two well known examples are the horrendous evil deeds of Hitler and Stalin.

3. Satan makes great efforts to persuade us to give ourselves to him

> "Now the serpent was more subtle than any other wild creature that the Lord God had made. He said to the woman, 'Did God say, "You shall not eat of any tree of the garden"?' And the woman said to the serpent, 'We may eat of the fruit of the trees of the garden; but God said, "You shall not eat of the fruit of the tree which is in the midst of the garden, neither shall you touch it, lest you die."' But the serpent said to the woman, 'You will not die. For God knows that when you eat of it your eyes will be opened, and you will be like God, knowing good and evil.'"

The advertising industry, a product of our modern society, is an excellent manifestation of the importance of our free decisions. This industry often works from the principle that the easiest way to get something you want from another human being is simply by encouraging him to give it to you. Billions of pounds are spent each year in an effort to convince people to make various kinds of decisions, each of which involves giving something of theirs, either money or votes. This approach works because there is always the implied promise of something more in return.[2]

With so much money at stake it is not surprising that the advertising industry has made great efforts to discover ways of influencing people's decisions. In particular, they seek ways to give people the impression that they are actually deciding freely, or 'on their own'.

Now, consider that, if the advertising industry puts so much effort into convincing people to give their money to product sponsors, how much more effort is Satan likely to expend in trying to convince us to give him, for his own selfish and destructive purposes, that which is the most precious of God's creations in this world – ourselves! Our decisions truly are important.

4. Decisions are two-edged swords

> "To Adam he said, 'Because you have listened to the voice of your wife, and have eaten of the tree of which I commanded you, "You shall not eat of it", cursed be the ground because of you; in toil you shall eat of it all the days of your life; thorns and thistles it shall bring forth to you; and you shall eat the plants of the field. In the sweat of your face you shall eat bread till you return to the ground."

Christ taught us to love our neighbour as ourselves. We must never ignore the fact that our decisions affect not only others, but also ourselves. Each decision we make is like a two-edged sword: it does something for, or to, others; and at the same time it does something for or to ourselves.

This principle is part of the mystery of being a human being, for the things that we do all contribute to what we become. God taught this to Adam and Eve 'in the beginning'. Their original sin illustrates the principle from the negative perspective: their sinful actions made them sinners – blocking their path to fulfilment, preventing them from living close to God[3]. The fact is that God has created each of us as a gift to our selves, and He has given us the ability to be a gift to others. Thus, the more we give of ourselves in ways that are in harmony with God's will, the more we will be in harmony with all that is good, and the greater a gift we will become. Ordinarily we do not see this process happening in ourselves, because it is a part of the mystery of God's love. We see the fruits later. But we can see it happening in others, especially in the lives of saints. We also know that when we refuse to be a gift for others (and thus give ourselves to Satan through sin), then we become less than the gift that we are called to be; and, as we become less, we have less to give to others.

These observations may be expressed, as a general principle, in terms of *privilege* and *responsibility*. It is our great privilege to have been given the gift of human life by God. As with every privilege, this gift of life comes with corresponding and balancing responsibilities. In particular, we are, as human beings, responsible not only for what we do, but also for what we become as a result of what we do.

For example, if, as I am walking home from work, I notice an elderly lady struggling to carry her groceries, I can decide to help her – that is, to give her the gift of myself through the gift of my time and energy. If I do so, then I am not only responsible for what I have done, but also for what I *become* as a result of my action. I have somehow become more of a gift as a result of that mysterious interaction between my actions and God's grace. Furthermore, one might say that by helping her I have become more of a loving, creative person, and so have become more of an image and likeness of God. As such I will, in turn, benefit others.

However, if I notice that the elderly lady has a hundred pounds in her purse, I can decide to steal it. If I do so, I am responsible not only for that action, but also for what I become as a result of doing it. In acting in this way, I have not given myself as a gift. Instead, I have taken that which is not mine, have acted selfishly, and destroyed a good which already existed. Thus, I have done something evil. As a result, I have impoverished myself as a gift, and become less generous and less able to love and be creative[4].

In other words, I am not being faithful to myself as a person made in the image and likeness of God. As with the first example, other people will be affected by this decision of mine; for, as a result of what I have become, I am less able to love them and creatively do the good which needs to be done.

This example may also help us to understand why we should never try to justify doing something we know is wrong by saying, "It doesn't affect anyone else". The reality is that *everything* we do, no matter how private, *does* affect others either directly or indirectly, because of what it does *to us* as gifts.

5. Privileges are balanced by corresponding responsibilities

> "The Lord God took the man and put him in the garden of Eden to till it and keep it. And the Lord God commanded the man, saying, 'You may freely eat of every tree of the garden; but of the tree of the knowledge of good and evil you shall not eat'."

As human beings, it is our great privilege to be able to make decisions. Each decision we make can be either to do good or to do evil; to be creative and loving, or selfish and destructive; to be faithful to the fact that we are made in the image and likeness of God, or to reject his call. But in accepting this great privilege of using our free will, we must be willing to assume the corresponding and balancing responsibilities.

Simply stated, these responsibilities are: to discover the truth, which God has given to us; and to choose to do the good which needs to be done in the light of that truth. Thus, for us to assume our true responsibilities as human beings, it is required that we use our intellect and free will *as they were intended to be used.*

III

THE SEARCH FOR WHAT IS TRUE

A. Introduction

Let us begin with some points that will guide us in making sound decisions. We must begin by *searching for the truth*, so that our decisions will be in harmony with the good which needs to be done.

We know from the first two chapters of Genesis that God took great care to teach us the important truths of life: He told Adam and Eve quite clearly what to eat and what not to eat, and what would happen if they disobeyed Him. He knew that without this knowledge, we would be unable to make free and sound decisions. He also knew that it was only with this knowledge that our decisions would be healthy ones, contributing in a positive way to all the relationships in which we have the privilege of being involved. The truths that God gave to Adam and Eve are still available to us today – and many more besides, because God came among us as Jesus Christ. But as a result of original sin we have to exert much more effort to make these truths our own. However, do not be put off by the need for effort – the results are well worth the struggle!

Let us now consider the following points, to assist us in our efforts to discover truth:

1. Objective Reality

In the search for what is true, it is a great asset to be aware that you are searching for what is called *objective reality*. What do these two words mean? They refer to that which exists, independently of what I think or desire. It is most important to grasp this point, because it helps you to realize that your goal is to *discover* what is, not to *create* it (God has already created all that is true and good). To attain this goal you must have an attitude of openness and of humility toward what exists – that is, toward the truth. Thus you must also be willing to call what is true, true, and what is not true, not true.[5]

The table on which my typewriter is resting is an example of an objective reality. It has an existence which does not depend upon my knowing or recognizing it. Whether I am in the room or not, and whether I admit its existence or not, the table still exists. Now, since both the table and I exist, I find myself in a real, objective (not subjective) relationship with it. If this relationship is to be a healthy one, then I must make the effort to discover certain truths about this table. I must use my intelligence to acquire knowledge of the truth; that is, I must try to have what is in my mind conform to what is in reality. Once there is sufficient harmony between what is in my mind and the objective reality of the table, a basis exists for a healthy relationship with it. This in turn enables good to be done. For example: I know that my table can be used not only to hold my typewriter, but I can also serve a meal on it; I also know that it is strong enough to bear my weight as I stand on it to change the bulb in the ceiling light.

2. Subjective Reality

It will help our understanding if we contrast objective reality with subjective reality. Subjective reality is that which exists only within my mind, that is, it has no existence outside of my mind.

We are all familiar with subjective reality. One common example is the young child who is afraid to put out his bedroom light because he thinks a monster will then immediately appear; another is the child who thinks that there is a real Santa Claus who slides down the chimney with a sack of presents at Christmas!

We all have this ability to generate images in our imaginations, and it can have some benefits. But we also must acquire the humility which helps us to realize that our thinking and willing something, does not cause it to *be*.

This fact must be emphasized. We have all been taught it and certainly apply it in our daily life, especially with regard to the material world. However, we tend to resist applying it to non-material areas, such as morality: what is right and wrong.

Let us look at some examples. We all know that, in order to drive a car, there must be some petrol in the tank. Simply thinking that the tank is full, or willing it to be so, does not make it so. Some learn this lesson the hard way when they run out of petrol and have to walk several miles to a petrol station before they can continue their journey!

This example illustrates the principle that there is a price to pay for acting only on the basis of what we call subjective reality. The principle applies to moral reality as well as to material reality. If a young woman thinks her fiancé is a single man, when in fact he is already married, that will not make him single. If she were to go through a marriage ceremony with him on the assumption that he is truly single, objectively she would not be married. The fact that she is not married is true even though she sincerely thinks she is.

Sincerity, by itself, is never enough: simply being sincere does not protect you from harm, nor does it protect you from harming yourself or others. Adam and Eve told themselves that eating the forbidden fruit was good, but we know that the results of their acting without the truth, *even if sincerely*, was disastrous. A young child is sincere in wanting to learn about the bright red object on the kitchen stove – the electric element. But if the child tries to learn by touching the element, his sincerity will not protect him from burning his hand. Each of these examples manifests the principle that sincerity without the truth can be very dangerous.

3. Teaching Children the Difference

Parents must be aware of the need to teach their children the difference between objective and subjective reality. This distinction is one of the great gifts parents can give their children. In so doing, they will be giving them an edge on true freedom because, as Christ teaches: "You shall know the truth and the truth will make you free" (Jn 8:32).

Parents have to teach their children this distinction, for example when they teach them that the hot electric element is not just a pretty thing to grasp, and that touching it will burn their hands and thereby limit their freedom. In this way, you teach your children not to enter into a touching relationship with the hot element, because it will not be a healthy and beneficial relationship for them.

Alternatively, consider the situation of a child who sees some coloured pills and, thinking they are sweets, wants to eat them. A parent observing this child will know that the child's thoughts are not in harmony with the reality of the pills. Consequently, the parent knows that if the child enters into an eating relationship with the pills, it will not be a healthy relationship for him. As a result, the parent says words to the effect of "No, you cannot eat those; they are not what you think they are, and they will harm you if you eat them". The parent will then try to explain to the child as much of the objective reality of the pills as the child can understand at that age.

In his early years, a child's knowledge of objective reality on various levels comes particularly through the faith and trust he has in his parents. Later, however, he will be able to verify the truth of what he has learned for himself.

Parents truly give their children a great gift by teaching them the difference between subjective and objective reality. The value of this gift is more immediately apparent on the material plane, but if they strive to teach their children that similar differences exist on the moral, spiritual and religious planes, then they will have given them an even greater gift. Parents should also always remember that, in teaching their children these truths, they are working in harmony with God, doing for their children what God did for Adam and Eve in the garden. Parents teach them the important truths in life – those truths which will give them freedom and provide them with the basis for healthy life-giving relationships.

Teaching their children these truths is one of the greatest privileges of being a parent, and the years parents have to teach each child are relatively short. It is important that parents do not waste those years, nor give them to someone else.

4. The Teenage Years

You will observe that most parents teach these material realities to their young children with a great deal of energy and confidence. But as the children become older, and especially when they reach their teens, many parents begin to lose their confidence and courage. They back off from teaching about objective reality, especially when they encounter strong emotional reactions to it in their children.

At times like these, they may have to pay a high price for teaching the truth; when a child is young, it is relatively easy to teach him about his limits, or that a lie is not in harmony with objective reality. But a teenage person often feels he has no limits, or believes that everything he thinks or wills is true, thus making the situation much more difficult.

At these times it is important not to back away from the truth of objective reality. When it is necessary to teach a teenager a new truth, or teach it to them again, parents must find new ways to do so. It may even mean asking someone outside the family to help – perhaps a priest, a teacher, or a family friend. Often teenagers do need to hear what parents know must be heard, but they need to hear it from someone who does not have the same emotional involvement with them as their parents.

Parents in this situation are often amazed to find that someone outside the family can say once what they have said many times before, and their child will act as if he had just heard it for the first time. Often the child responds by saying, "Hey, this makes sense". At such times parents are wise to be quiet and, in humility, say a prayer of thanks. Their silence at this time will be the good which needs to be done to help their child inform his conscience on the matter in question.

B. Assistance in the Search (1)

1. Who to ask

Experience with life teaches us that even as adults we often need to ask the help of others in our search for objective reality. For example, it is common to seek advice in the areas of car repairs and bodily health. As a result, we quite readily turn to mechanics and doctors for assistance in determining objective reality, so that we can make good decisions in these matters.

Let us consider first the case of the mechanic. There are good mechanics and bad ones. The difference lies in the ability of the good mechanic to discover the objective reality of a malfunctioning car, i.e. what is *really* wrong with it. With this information, he can make a sound judgement about what to do next. His ability allows him to provide us with a valuable service: one for which we are willing to pay. Experience shows that by taking the trouble to ascertain the objective reality about one's car, one can avoid many future problems, save a great deal of money, and often save lives.

The poor mechanic, for whatever reason, does not have the ability to discover what is really wrong with a car: the objective reality. As a result he must guess at the cause of the problem. Such a mechanic operates on the basis of his subjective reality. Because there is a lack of harmony between what is in his mind and the objective problem with the car, decisions made on the basis of his advice cannot be sound. They will not be good for the car, nor for the client's wallet. If the client continues to return to the poor mechanic, more money, and perhaps even lives, will be lost.

What we have said about mechanics is also true of medical doctors. When a patient who is in pain comes to a good doctor, the doctor uses his skills to discover the real cause of the problem, i.e. what the objective reality is. Having discovered this, he can suggest what needs to be done to correct the problem. Then the patient will know what is truly wrong, and he can make sound decisions, have a good medical relationship with the doctor, and receive treatment to restore his health. On the other hand, we know what happens when a patient is treated by a doctor who only guesses at what is wrong! He is convinced that his guess is the reality, and bases his decisions upon it.

Both the medical profession and the state are acutely aware of how important it is that those involved in treating patients be able to ascertain objective medical reality. We, too, need to be aware of its importance on the moral level and obtain sufficient training to be able to recognise it.

2. The Need for Trust

We know from experience that a certain degree of *trust* is required as part of the relationship with the mechanic or the doctor. This trust is especially necessary if the client has not been trained in the relevant field, and so may not fully understand the explanation he is given. A good doctor or mechanic confirms this trust and builds it up for the future by giving good results. This process of evaluation is part of what Christ is teaching when he says: "By their fruits you will know them" (Mt 7:16).

C. Assistance in the Search (2)

1. Moral, Spiritual, and Religious Realities

There is an objective reality in the moral, spiritual and religious realms of life. In these realms as in the others, sound decisions are required if we are to form healthy relationships with God and our neighbour. You can appreciate that it is more difficult to discover objective reality in these areas than it is in the areas of mechanics or medicine. We must also be aware that, in these realms, we are more likely to equate our subjective reality with objective reality. However, the fact that it is difficult to find does not make the objective reality any less real. It simply means that we will need to seek help more often, and from those who are trained in discovering objective reality in these areas. Once found, it will set us free.

We saw how, in the beginning, God helped Adam and Eve to know objective truth. And now, since the disaster of original sin, the need for this knowledge is even greater. For one of the effects of original sin was to dim our ability to see objective truth in these, less visual, areas of reality.

2. Who to ask

When seeking moral and religious advice in these areas, you should apply the same principles which you apply in searching for a good mechanic or doctor. A good spiritual director or pastor, for example, is able to show you objective reality (spiritual, moral, and intellectual), because he knows, through his training and his experience, how to discover it (just as does the good doctor in his field). In contrast, a poor spiritual director relies on, for example, guesses and current opinions. Consequently his advice is based mainly on subjective reality. As in medicine, subjective reality does not provide a secure basis for decisions which are meant to contribute to sound, strong, spiritual and moral health. Such direction usually results in your being subjected to various kinds of techniques, depending on what is fashionable at the time.

As your life continues, you will have occasion to seek help in discovering the objective reality concerning various questions in these areas of life. Choose a good spiritual director to help you. You have a responsibility to search for and consult with those who work on the basis of objective reality. The truth they show you, you can trust.

3. Comparing his Advice to God's

One method that helps in assessing whether or not a spiritual director is advising you on the basis of objective reality, is to compare what he says with what God has already taught us, for example, in the Ten Commandments. If his advice would mean breaking one of the Commandments, then you can be certain that he is working on the level of subjective reality, and will not be able to provide good help. God's law, as given in the Ten Commandments, and through Jesus Christ, is the surest guide to objective reality.

It is helpful to remember always that sincerity, by itself, whether in you or in the one whom you ask for help, is not sufficient. By itself, sincerity cannot provide the basis for decisions which will produce creative, loving actions in harmony with God's own creative, loving actions.

D. Use your Free Will

So far we have concentrated on deepening our appreciation of objective reality by saying what it is, why it is important, and why you should make an effort to discover it before making decisions. We have mentioned factors which can help you in your search, and others which you would do well to avoid, since they can only hinder you. However, one important lesson we need to learn in this life is that the truth must be approached with an attitude of *humility*, for we are called to discover it – not to invent or create it.

We all lean naturally towards the good, and our will encourages our intellect to seek what is good. Thus the good can, in a sense, be chosen and possessed. In doing this we remain faithful to ourselves as beings made in the image and likeness of God.

I emphasise these points because I wish to encourage you strongly: always use this great gift of freedom to choose the good that needs to be done. Do not allow your feelings to rule your intellect, or else they will become the directing force of your free will.

IV

AN INFORMED CONSCIENCE

A. The Person

I would like to begin this section with some reflections on the significance of the human person, since it is the human person who informs his conscience. I will offer these reflections with the help of a diagram, and hopefully a little humour.

When a young lady, Jill, first sees an attractive young man, Tim, could one say that she sees what is in the diagram below?

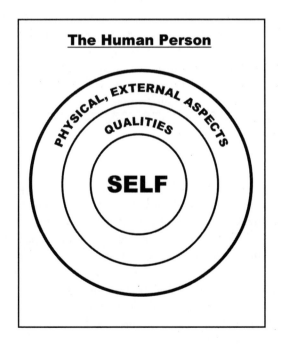

1. Externals

Let us begin with the outer circle, which represents a certain level of knowledge about Tim. We will then gradually move inwards, as indicated by the increasingly smaller circles which represent other levels of knowledge of the person.

This first circle represents what Jill sees when she first becomes aware of Tim, that is, his external or physical appearance. This dimension includes, for example, how tall he is, the colour of his eyes and hair, and what he is wearing. It is normal to be aware of this physical dimension, because the first information we observe and record whenever we meet another human being, is his or her visible appearance and other external facts. This has certainly been the pattern since Adam first saw Eve. We are created as body-persons, and so the external dimensions of the body present themselves first to the senses, especially vision and hearing.

We tend to collect this information automatically, even though we are always aware that there is more to a person than meets the eye. With an attitude of openness, we will be able to learn some of that 'more'. If Jill has this attitude when she first meets Tim, good things can be built on the natural attractions of external appearances.

2. Lust

Of course, if we do not have a positive attitude of openness to the 'more' in another, and a willingness to discover it, we tend (at least mentally) to reduce the other to his external factors and attractions. We thus essentially reduce the other person to an object. Since objects are things to use, it is then tempting to think of ways we might use the person. Once this thought arises, the foundation is laid for lust. Lust is a vice[6]. In its simplest form it is an act of *devouring* another as an object – either mentally or sensually. Obviously, this attitude is to be avoided in human relationships and especially in a marriage and a family. The excitement a newly engaged couple feels comes from their knowing that each has been chosen by the other, not as an object, but for the *total person* that he or she is. This realisation should strengthen both members of the couple in their love and their intention never to treat one other as objects. It will also help them eventually to give their future children a better early preparation for marriage and family.

3. Natural Attraction to the Good

Remember, too, that when God created us, He created us very good. As a result, we have what might be called a natural attraction to the good. When we meet another human being, we experience him at the level of outward appearances, and so it is at this level that the attraction to the good begins. We saw that, before original sin, because of God's grace, Adam had the ability to see not only the external good of the other (Eve), but also her *total good* – all in the first glance (cf. Gen 2:23). Since original sin, however, we must constantly strive, one step at a time, to reach this same point. So when we find ourselves attracted to the external good in another person, we should be encouraged to discover more of the good that is *in* the person. This is of course a great compliment to the other!

In contrast, the person who reduces the other to a mere object is saying, in effect, "The only good here is what meets my eye". Obviously, this belief is grossly untrue and a great insult to both the other person and to God, who created and redeemed that person.

B. The Person's Qualities

In our example, Jill has this positive attitude of openness toward Tim: she is open to discovering more of the good in him, which means that she is open to learning more about who he really is. Therefore, she decides to stay around and come to know him better.

As Jill gets to know Tim, she soon discovers some of the goodness expressed in qualities he has developed, for example, his ability to sing, to cook, to organise, to make people laugh, to play tennis, to skate and to teach Scripture (isn't he great!). This time of discovery can be rather fascinating and exciting – a special excitement is always added to human relationships when good things are discovered about the other. Adam too felt this excitement when he first saw Eve and discovered her truth and goodness (cf. Gen 2:23).

1. Infatuation

While this excitement remains good in this context, it is important that we understand it properly: it is usually what we call *infatuation*, and should not be mistaken for authentic love. Infatuation does assist in the discovery of the good of the other person, but it lacks that enduring quality essential to authentic love. Consequently, no lasting relationship, such as marriage, should ever be based on mere infatuation – it has to develop into *true* love.

2. Qualities are not the Person

Unfortunately, some couples try to build a marriage on this foundation, thinking that admiration for a person's qualities is real love. A few years later, many find themselves asking, "Is this the person I married?" The reason is that the *qualities* an individual has do not equal the *person*; they are simply ways in which the person expresses himself. Consequently, they can change with circumstances, even though the person himself remains the same.

Qualities are also means by which a person tries to be creative and do good in the various situations in which he finds himself. We are emphasising good qualities; a person can also develop negative qualities such as selfishness. Discovering such qualities in a person would indicate that he or she is not ready for marriage.

Experience teaches that life often presents us with new situations: they require a creative response, if we are to do the good which needs to be done. By learning to respond in this way, we often develop new qualities. This is very evident to parents as they respond to the needs (the 'good which needs to be done') of their growing children. Later these parents will discover that, in responding to these needs, they themselves have become more patient and generous, have learned to drive, to teach catechism, and so on.

We should enjoy the excitement of the process of discovering the good in other persons, and encourage its development. But we must not make the mistake of thinking that the qualities of a person are the person himself. Parents should have the same attitude towards their children, for there is much good to discover in them – they should rejoice and be excited by the good qualities they find, but they should not mistake a child's qualities for the person that child is.

The fact that a person is not his qualities is dramatically brought home to us when an debilitating illness strikes and drastically alters a person's means of self-expression. At such a time, we either penetrate to the core of the person's goodness and respond to that in love, or we turn away from him.

It is important for parents to teach these basic truths to their children. Let them learn in their own home how to make the basic distinctions between a person's qualities and the person himself. By understanding this distinction they will wisely choose their future spouse and will thank their parents for this gift of discernment later in life.

C. The Person's Inner Core

Look back at the diagram on page 23. In order to move from the second circle, which represents a person's qualities, to the third circle, you need respect, humility and patience. This third circle represents the inner or true self. When you know this, you know the person. The inner self of another is not something you can take; rather, it is a kind of hidden and precious gift which must be freely given by the person to whom it belongs. (This attitude is most important in marriage.) You must learn to wait with respect and humble patience before this mystery is revealed.

It is when this gift is given that one begins to touch the core (or foundation) of the human being. When you see it, you are privileged to see and experience more clearly the truth, goodness and beauty of that person, and begin to glimpse the gift of God which he or she is.

I use the terms *truth*, *goodness*, and *beauty* because, as we know, each person is a special creation of God, and whatever God creates has these three things: truth, goodness and beauty. This means that each person is a unique, creative 'word' spoken by God, a word which in fact He will never speak again. That is how special each person is. In this sense there can never be a substitute for any individual human person. The gift of each person does not allow for comparison. Therefore it is a waste of time to compare yourself to others on this level of gift.

1. Truth, Goodness and Beauty
Let us return to these three terms and develop their meaning as

they apply to the self. Returning to our example, Tim is God's spoken creative word. Since God's word is always true, there is in Tim's very being, the special truth of *who* and *what* he is. God's word is always good, so there is also a special and basic goodness of who and what Tim is. This special goodness is his, from the very beginning of his existence. We also know that God's creative word radiates beauty, because it is from the union of truth and goodness that real beauty is born. Thus Tim has his own inner beauty as a unique, creative, spoken word of God; it is his own unique beauty born from the union of his own unique truth and goodness. The same is true of each one of us. It is true of every child God gives to a family, and it is very important to teach these truths to children.

We must remember that original sin affects each of us from the time of conception; this tendency towards evil obscures our ability to see another person clearly. The fact that the gift of another person is not immediately apparent, however, does not mean that it does not exist.

We also know that we have been given the gifts of intelligence and free will. We can either use these gifts to build on the truth, goodness and beauty which have been given to us especially in our creation and redemption, or we can use them in a way which takes away from the truth. This choice reflects a deeper dimension of what was explained above, i.e., that we are responsible not only for what we do, but also for what we *become* as a result of what we do.

We also face this choice with respect to one another: we can help each other to be faithful to the truth, goodness and beauty that is ours, and thus help each other to grow in the image and likeness of God; or we can lead others to be unfaithful, and thus be destructive of themselves as God's image and likeness. Marriage and family certainly require a commitment on the part of husband and wife to do the former, both for each other, and for their children. Children must also be taught how to help each other in this same way.

The words of Isaiah, the prophet, may help you in your reflections on this point. Isaiah relates God's prophetic word to us, as he says: "For as the rain and the snow come down from heaven, and do not return without watering the earth, making it yield and giving growth to provide seed to the sower and bread to the eater, so shall my word be, that goes forth from my mouth; it shall not return to me empty, but it shall accomplish that which I propose, and prosper in the things for which I sent it" (Is 55:10–11).

For example, we discover part of the truth of who a person is when we discover what God has called him to do. At present, God may be calling Tim and Jill into the rich harvest of marriage, to do a great deal of good within their own marriage and family for the Church and the world. Like the gentle rain that comes down from heaven and does good for the soil, for the plants and thus for mankind, so Tim and Jill can do a great deal of good on this earth before they return to Him from whom they first came.

D. Love's Foundation: The Person

Love finds its foundation in this *permanent core* of the person. You can verify this dimension of permanency for yourself. Simply meditate on your own past reflections on yourself. Think back to when you were three and reflected on yourself, when you were six, twelve and eighteen. At each moment in the past it was always the same you who was doing the reflecting. As the years have passed, you have grown physically, intellectually, emotionally, and spiritually, but the person reflecting is still the same you. It is this person, the rock of stability, which is your true core. In our relationships with others, as with ourselves, we must always be faithful to this truth.

In particular, the relationship of marriage must build lasting love on this basis. The love of spouses must be for the person himself; they must love the other person's own special truth, goodness and beauty. When you love in this way it gives a proper perspective for understanding and adjusting to any outward changes which may take place over the years, especially those which come with advancing age or illness. It is a form of ongoing conversion.

When you love in this way it also gives you more confidence in facing the future together. This is because the inner beauty of a person is meant to increase with advancing years, even though the exterior beauty may fade. Consequently, when a person is loved in this way there is no need to fear competition from the external beauty of youth. Spouses must help each other to develop this inner beauty, and grow in their ability to recognise it in each other. In other words, they must strive to see each other *through God's eyes*.

E. Teaching Children

Parents, as you help your children to inform their consciences, be certain to teach them of their unconditional worth. This resides in their own unique truth, goodness and beauty, which has been created by the Father and redeemed by the Son. Teach them also the source of their own beauty: God and his grace. Teach them how to accept themselves, and to let the inner beauty which is theirs radiate. They will find that not only does it transform the outer levels, but it also nourishes the inner ones.

The late Mother Teresa exemplifies this truth. From the time God put her on the world stage, as a model of charity, until her death, her physical appearance would never have won her a Miss Universe beauty title. But she was considered by most people

who met her (including the late Princess Diana) to be the most beautiful person they had ever met. Why? Because over the years she co-operated with God and his grace in developing the inner beauty which was hers, and this shone outwardly in a way that all could see. What a marvellous freedom this gave her! She was not concerned whether others approved of her physical appearance or her ability to entertain or sing, or pass exams. She was free from the control that the world often exercises on people, who depend upon the approval of others of their beauty and skills. Her freedom allowed her true self to blossom in the love of God and Neighbour.

If parents give their children this same gift of freedom, then they too will become 'something beautiful for God', and for others!

F. God

1. Our Helper

Let us now put God explicitly into our diagram. We will put Him in two places: first outside the circles, and then at the heart of the inner circle. We do this to show, firstly, that in His relationship with us He is both separate from us *and* very close to us; secondly that, because God is Truth, Goodness and Beauty, He wants to relate to us in our own truth, goodness and beauty, which He has given to us through creation and redemption.

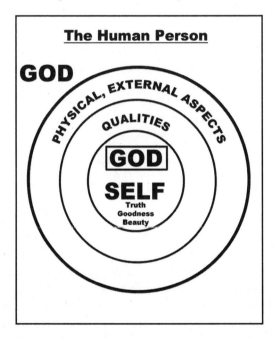

(a) **Within the person:** We may be tempted to keep God at a distance, offering Him only the other two levels of ourselves. For example, we might say, "I will go to Church on Sunday, Lord, and put on a new suit just for you to look at, but please don't look at what is deep within my heart!" Or, "I will go and sing in the choir and give you one of my qualities each Sunday, but please don't ask me to give you my heart". But true love is never satisfied with externals, and so God, our Redeemer, wants to be invited into our inner sanctuary and there to relate to the *total person* that we each are.

It is here, in this inner sanctuary, that we make our personal decisions. In this inner sanctuary we can make our moral decisions with God and, in a sense, in front of Him. To do so in this way gives us a great advantage: it makes available to us the best possible Counsellor to assist us in making sound decisions – for example, about what is right and wrong, or what needs to be done in order to grow in love.

The Second Vatican Council expressed this well in its teaching on conscience. It says: "Conscience is the most secret core of a man. There he is alone with God, whose voice echoes in his depths." [7]

(b) Outside the person: In our diagram, God is also placed *outside* the three circles, to emphasise the fact that He speaks to us and helps us from outside as well as from within. This is especially important in a world spoiled by original sin, because there is another who also tries to speak to us from within. He speaks especially to our intellect, in his attempts to deceive us as to what is true and what is not. And so God has given us a means of checking the truth of what we hear within – by comparing it with what God has said externally; for example, in the Ten Commandments. We know that if what we hear from within is not in harmony with what God has said outside, then we should disregard what we hear inside because it is not from Him. We need to do this for the good of our moral health, both temporal and eternal. There is a fundamental principle at work here, of which we can be absolutely certain: God does not contradict Himself!

2. God does not contradict himself

We can see an excellent application of this principle by the Virgin Mary herself in St. Luke's Gospel (1:26–38). The angel Gabriel appeared to her within her frame of reference, that is, in a visible form. He claimed to offer her the opportunity to do a great deal of good for God and for the whole world. As she listened to what the angel said, she was disturbed: he seemed to be telling her that she would become a mother *now*, in her virginal state. Mary certainly knew enough reproductive biology to know that this could not be done without violating God's commandments. And so she asked that very wise and penetrating question: "How can this be, since I have no husband?" (v. 34). Then the angel Gabriel explained that it would be done by means of God's own creative power – the same power by which He created the world. Having informed her conscience in this way, she knew that it was not Satan but God himself who was asking this of her, and so she freely chose to say 'yes' to Him. She freely chose to give God the gift of herself so that He could do good things with her – and through her, God gave her and us the incredible gift of Jesus Christ, our Lord and Saviour.

Eve and Adam could have saved themselves and all of us a lot of heartache if they had applied this same principle in the Garden of Eden when Satan offered them what appeared to be an opportunity to do good things. For in this case, it was quite apparent that, in order to accomplish the 'good' suggested by Satan ("your eyes will be opened, and you will be like God, knowing good and evil"), they would have to disobey God ("You shall not eat of the fruit of the tree which is in the midst of the garden, neither shall you touch it, lest you die").

G. How God Helps Externally

1. The Total Vision of Man

(a) **External Sources:** Our diagram (page 33) helps us to see that God, in his mercy, is doing a great deal to help us to inform our conscience. He has made known to us all that we need to know in order to be true to ourselves and to Him, in all of our decisions and actions. He is constantly encouraging us to make those decisions which are in harmony with Him. God is not indifferent to us. However, He does not take the responsibilities which are ours. Since we have the privilege of making decisions, we must also assume the corresponding and balancing responsibilities. These include gathering the necessary information (from that which God has made available), so that we can discover the objective reality of the situations we encounter, and thus make healthy, life-giving decisions. If God were to assume this responsibility for us, we would be put out of balance, because we would then be exercising a privilege without accepting the corresponding and balancing responsibilities. And God certainly would not do this to us.

Thus, in assuming our responsibility in this area, we should be prepared to do our homework. This means seeking information from five basic sources:

(i) human nature;
(ii) the wisdom of the ages;
(iii) our reason;
(iv) scripture;
(v) the teaching and wisdom of the Church.

These efforts should be accompanied by prayer and ongoing conversion.

Now, on our diagram, we will connect each source of information with the inner circle (that is, the core of the person) with a line. This line represents the person's efforts to discover the necessary information from these sources in order to make a decision.

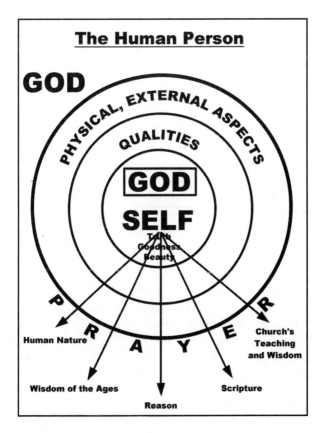

Let us illustrate this search by means of an example: a first-year university student discovers that she is pregnant, and the university doctor who gave her this information recommends that she have an abortion. He suggests to her that there is nothing wrong with an abortion, since the foetus is not yet a human being. The woman and her boyfriend go to the pastor for advice.

At this point the pastor's task is to help them realise that the first question is *not* whether to have an abortion or not, but rather, "What is the objective reality of an abortion?" That is, "What is the meaning of such an action?" In order to answer this question, one must then ask: "What is actually in her womb? Is there a human being there or not?" Let us approach these questions using the five sources of information mentioned above:

(i) **Knowledge of Human Nature:** We begin to answer these questions by seeking information from the first source: our knowledge of human nature. This includes all scientific information which is now available. A study of this material shows that a new human being exists from the time of conception. For example, the late Dr Jérôme Lejeune, who was one of the world's leading geneticists, stated very firmly that it is a biological fact that "human life begins at conception". [8]

(ii) **The Wisdom of the Ages:** The second source of information is the wisdom of the ages. In other words, what have we, the human race, learned from our years of history and observation about this question of the child in the womb? In particular, what have we learned from our mistakes, i.e. abortion? The abortions themselves continually reveal to us that it is a human being in the mother's womb.

(iii) **Our Reason:** The third source of information comes from using our reason. Our reason was given to us by God, and He wants us to use it to understand truth and to call it by its name. This also means using our reason to understand better the content of sources (i) and (ii), and to try to gain new insights into the truth of the child in the womb. We cannot rely only on feelings for this understanding; we must use our intellect. And, as a result of this effort at understanding, we may find that new insights develop.

(iv) **Scripture:** Scripture provides a fourth and very important source of information for informing our consciences, since it often shows us truths which we either are not able to see or do not see clearly on our own – for example, the truth that it is good to "Love your enemy" (Mt 5:44). With respect to the question of whether human life exists in the womb, scripture shows us the truth in St Luke's account of Mary's visit to Elizabeth. Only a few days after Mary conceived (by the power of the Holy Spirit), Elizabeth, inspired by that same Holy Spirit, recognised the presence of a new human being in Mary's womb (Lk 1:39–45). The scriptures are an important source of information for us, since original sin has affected our ability to see beyond appearances. And so, through scripture, God provides us with the assistance of what we might call divine clarity.

(v) **The Teaching Authority of the Church:** Christ himself speaks to us through the teaching authority of his Church. This gives us our fifth source of information, one which for Catholics is very important. It was entrusted to the Apostles and their successors to preserve and hand on what Christ had taught. They were also given the task of guiding the followers of Christ in applying these teachings to new situations as they arose. We also know that Christ gave us the Holy Spirit, the Spirit of Truth, to ensure that the truth is always available to us. Furthermore, the Spirit of Truth stands against the spirit of untruth, so that the gates of Hell cannot prevail against Christ's Church (cf. Mt 16:18 and Acts 2:1ff). Christ has given us so much through the Church. Through her He gave us the Scriptures of the New Testament, and a guarantee of the Old Testament and the Spirit of Truth who guides the Church in her authentic interpretation of the Scriptures. Consequently the Church has much to teach us about objective reality (truth) because Christ himself *is* Truth.

If we return to the question of when human life begins, we can receive guidance from the Church's teaching of the dogma of the Immaculate Conception. Essentially this dogma says that Mary was conceived by her parents, Anna and Joachim, free from original sin and full of grace. Faith and reason teach us that only a *person* can be free from sin and full of grace. Therefore, the dogma of the Immaculate Conception only makes sense if Mary was created a human person at the moment of conception. She confirmed this truth at Lourdes (1858) when she said to St Bernadette, "I am the Immaculate Conception". The Immaculate Conception thus confirms with divine clarity that a human person is created at the moment of conception.

The gift of faith enables us to benefit from this divine clarity. As a theological virtue, faith elevates our intellect's ability to know *with* God – i.e. God himself knows that He has created a new person at the moment of conception, and through faith we come to share in that knowledge. Faith also strengthens our will in saying yes, I believe, to what we have come to know with God. "By faith, man completely submits his intellect and his will to God." [9]

In this and various other ways, the Catholic Church fulfils its role of service to the truth. Vatican II expressed it in the following way: "The Catholic Church is, by the will of Christ, the teacher of truth. It is Her duty to proclaim and teach with authority the truth which is Christ, and at the same time, to declare and confirm by Her authority the principles of the moral order which spring from 'human nature' itself." [10]

(b) The Internal Source: After having gathered information from all these sources, we must take it into the core of our person, where we can put it together by means of our own reasoning. We should also discuss it with God, which means coming to God in prayer. All of these efforts help to clarify the picture of the objective reality we are seeking. Once the picture is sufficiently clarified, then we have informed our conscience.

H. The Conscience Informed

1. Responding to Objective Reality

Let us now return to the pregnant university student and her friend. After having informed their conscience as described above, they know with certainty that a new human being exists within her womb. This is the objective reality; once it is accepted, it automatically raises another question: "How will we relate to this new person? Will we be generous and creative or selfish and destructive?" To have an abortion would be to act selfishly and destructively: it would be, in fact, to destroy another human being's life. To respond positively means to ask, "What is the good which needs to be done for this new person we have discovered?" From the perspective of the gospel, a new neighbour has been discovered – a neighbour in need. For the present, while he is in his mother's womb, the needs of this new neighbour are simple: a bit of nourishment, some warmth and shelter, a space for exercise and a bit of time to grow. The only one able to respond to these basic needs is the young woman within whose womb the new neighbour is now living. One would hope that support and encouragement would also come from the biological father, the parents' families and from society.

Even if support does not come from these quarters, however, the objective reality of the good which needs to be done for this new neighbour remains the same. Such a situation serves to emphasise the fact that truly loving one's neighbour often requires effort and sacrifice. Christ himself made great efforts and sacrifices to love us in our need of salvation.

At this point the two people have also informed their consciences as to the good which needs to be done for their new neighbour. With this solid knowledge, they each stand before God, in that inner circle, to decide whether to do the good or not. God also stands with them to encourage them to love their new neighbour, as He himself does.

(a) Loving and Creative: If the decision is 'yes', then everyone benefits. Not only will the new neighbour benefit and grow from this decision, but so will all the others who know the couple. For that decision will help to make the couple more creative and loving. In saying 'yes' to this new life, they have chosen to follow Christ more closely – who gave his life that we might live.

(b) Selfish and Destructive: On the other hand, the couple, after having informed their conscience, may choose not to love their new neighbour, but to have an abortion. If so, they will definitely know what they have done. Since they know, there is the possibility of repentance in the future and thus a turning back to God for forgiveness and inner healing. If instead they had followed the doctor's initial advice and proceeded, thinking (subjectively) that no human being existed in the womb, the results would have been the same for the new neighbour – he would have been destroyed. And objectively this destruction of the child would have eaten away at their own truth, goodness and beauty, because what they did was contrary to their having been created in the image and likeness of God. Such an act leaves deep inner wounds; these can only be healed by acceptance of the objective reality, repentance and asking forgiveness from God. Without an informed conscience, the couple are deprived of that opportunity, and may suffer for years before discovering the reality and the cure they need.

One is very much aware of this problem as a confessor. Sometimes it is only five, ten, or even twenty years later that the person's conscience is finally properly informed on such a matter. When this happens and they seek the confessional, the results can be amazing. But sometimes that search for the truth is delayed by seeking help from the wrong sources. For example, there was a woman who, five years after her abortion, was beginning to suspect the source of her interior problems. She went to a psychiatrist who did not believe in God. This doctor later said to me (without revealing any names): "I don't know why she has a problem. I told her that she got rid of it five years ago." Sad to say, five years before, when she aborted her child, she did not get rid of her 'problem'. Rather, the abortion was the cause of the enormous problem she now had.

I mention these examples to emphasise how terribly important it is for each of us to make the effort to discover objective reality, even to the point of making sacrifices to this end. For only by doing this can we understand the real meaning of what we intend to do or of what we have already done. Once again we see that it is the truth which sets us free.

V

CONCLUSION

The whole process which we have described (searching out the objective reality and discovering the real meaning of our actions, either those which we intend or those which are in the past) is what we call informing our conscience.

It is a rightly informed conscience which the Church teaches us to follow. This is because, if a person informs his conscience properly, that is, in the way we have explained above, then he will discover the truth and will be following the truth. And the truth becomes the pathway to God.

I would emphasise that it is an *informed* conscience which we are to follow – not just our conscience. Conscience by itself does not create truth, nor is it an oracle which proclaims truth. Rather, it enables us to work in harmony with truth, and in this way to be true to our dignity as human beings, made in the image and likeness of God.

There are many who claim to follow their conscience but who, at the same time, lack an understanding of what it means to have an informed conscience. As a result, they often end up following the guidance of subjective reality (for example, their feelings, or what everybody else is saying or doing). This eventually leads them down the path walked by Adam and Eve.

We are meant to be about something very important, when we make the effort to inform our conscience. We may emphasise this by reflecting on the two Latin words from which the word *conscience* is formed: *con* and *scientia*, meaning *with* and *knowledge* (from the root, *scire*, i.e. *to know*). In this sense, our conscience is for knowing *with* someone, and the one we really want to know with is God. Thus, to make the effort to inform one's conscience is to make the effort to come to know with God. And if I come to know with Him, then I can walk with Him as a friend, and together we can walk into eternity.

Let us look back at 'the beginning' from this perspective. In the beginning, Adam and Eve knew with God, and so walked with Him 'in the cool of the evening' (in biblical language, this is the time shared with good friends). Later, they decided to know with someone else, namely, Satan. We know the results of this decision: you walk with the one with whom you know, and make decisions with Him. Adam and Eve no longer knew with God and so no longer walked with Him. Again, we see the true importance of informing our conscience: it is absolutely necessary if we are to walk with the right person, who is Truth, Life and Love, in all things.

Conscience formation is an ongoing process of searching for and discovering objective truth and meaning. God has provided and continues to provide what we need. But we must have an attitude of openness to the truth, which means a certain humility – for we are discovering truth, not creating it. St Augustine expresses it well in his *Confessions*, when he says, "[God,] You answer clearly, yet not everyone hears clearly. All ask what they wish, but do not hear what they wish. He serves you best who aims not to hear from you what he wishes, but to will whatever he hears from you." [11] An Indian proverb expresses this truth in another way: "To him who will not accept the truth as a friend, it comes as a conqueror".

In many respects our conscience is a reminder of our dignity and freedom, and how very much God respects both. We have the ability to know whomever we choose, and thus to walk with whomever we choose. God respects our choice and its consequences, but He is not indifferent. He has done and continues to do a great deal to help us to know Him, who is love, so that we can walk with Him. There are countless examples of this throughout salvation history: the saints, who can be our help and prayerful inspiration as we strive to make the right choices which will lead us to everlasting life with God.

NOTES

1 Cf. Second Vatican Council, *Gaudium et Spes*, §24.
2 More often, though, advertising is used not simply to inform but to persuade and motivate – to convince people to act in certain ways: to buy certain products or services. (*Ethics in Advertising*, Pontifical Council for Social Communications, 25 February, 1999).
3 Cf. Second Vatican Council, *Gaudium et Spes*, §13.
4 Cf. *ibid*.
5 Cf. St Thomas Aquinas, *Summa Theologiae*, I, 20, 2.
6 Cf. *Catechism of the Catholic Church*, §2351.
7 Second Vatican Council, *Gaudium et Spes*, §16.
8 As quoted in Andras Tehan, *A Case of Life and Death: The Trial of the Century* (Battleford, Sask.; Marian Press, 1983) p.26.
9 Cf. *Catechism of the Catholic Church*, §143.
10 Second Vatican Council, *Dignitatis Humanae*, §14. In matters of faith and morals the Catholic knows that the sign of any teacher's authenticity is the harmony which exists between his teaching and that of the Church, as expressed by the Pope. If that harmony is lacking, then the Catholic is wise to say to such a teacher, "Thanks, but no thanks". This principle has been used to evaluate even some pastors and bishops over the centuries; for, unfortunately, some pastors and bishops have taught heresies, and had heresies named after them. But no Pope, as Pope, has ever taught a heresy or had one named after him.
11 As quoted in *A Short Breviary* (Collegeville, Minn.; St John's Abbey Press, 1975), p 217.

SUGGESTED FURTHER READING

Marriage Preparation:
A Catholic Handbook for Engaged and Newly Married Couples,
F W Marks. Emmaus Road. ISBN 1-931018-01-4
Good News About Sex and Marriage, Christopher West. Charis.
Journey of Faith: Catholic Marriage Preparation, Roy Barkley. Queenship
ISBN 1-57918-179-1

Morality, Conscience, etc:
Authority and Conscience, ed. Denis Riches. Family Publications.
ISBN 1-871217-18-0
Catechism of the Catholic Church (part 3)
Crisis of Conscience, ed. John M Haas. Crossroad Herder.
Living the Catechism of the Catholic Church, Vol. 3, Christoph Cardinal
Schönborn. Ignatius Press. ISBN 0-89870-835-4
A Refutation of Moral Relativism, Peter Kreeft. Ignatius Press.
ISBN 0-89870-731-5

Marriage and Theology of the Body
Crossing the Threshold of Love, Mary Shivanandan. T&T Clark.
Love and Responsibility, Karol Wojtyla. Ignatius. ISBN 0-89870-445-0
Marriage: Mystery of Faithful Love, Dietrich von Hildebrand. Sophia
Institute Press. ISBN 0-918477-00-X
Marriage: the Rock, William May. Ignatius. ISBN 0-89870-537-1
Theology of the Body, John Paul II. Pauline.
Three Approaches to Abortion, P Kreeft. Ignatius. ISBN 0-89870-915-6
Why Humanae Vitae Was Right, ed. Janet Smith. Ignatius.
ISBN 0-89870-433-2

For teenagers and young adults:
Desiderata: a Teenager's Journey to God, David P Eich. Ignatius.
ISBN 0-89870-858-3
Real Love, Mary Beth Bonacci. Ignatius. ISBN 0-89870-613-0

**All of the above titles can be obtained (subject to availability)
from Family Publications, 6a King Street, Oxford. OX2 6DF.**